THE
JEWEL BOX
BIOGRAPHIES

STEPHEN A. KLOTZ

Copyright © 2021 Stephen A. Klotz

All rights reserved. No part of this book may be reproduced, stored, or transmitted by any means—whether auditory, graphic, mechanical, or electronic—without written permission of both publisher and author, except in the case of brief excerpts used in critical articles and reviews. Unauthorized reproduction of any part of this work is illegal and is punishable by law.

ISBN: 978-1-957203-23-2 (sc)
ISBN: 978-1-957203-24-9 (hc)
ISBN: 978-1-957203-25-6 (e)

Because of the dynamic nature of the Internet, any web addresses or links contained in this book may have changed since publication and may no longer be valid. The views expressed in this work are solely those of the author and do not necessarily reflect the views of the publisher, and the publisher hereby disclaims any responsibility for them.

The Ewings Publishing LLC
One Galleria Blvd., Suite 1900, Metairie, LA 70001
1-888-421-2397

CONTENTS

Where Are They Now? 1
Clark, the Forerunner 3
Mario the Painter 7
Captain Hill 12
Jon the Coquette 15
Lauren the Blasphemer 18
The Jewel Box 21
Reverend Steven, Tele-Evangelist 24
Wayne: The Man who Would not Eat 26
Eddie and the 7th Street Bridge 30
Debbie, Robert and Stimpy 33
Buckaroo with a Shapely Bottom 35
Tony and Gary 37
Son of a Bitch Emmit 40
Kendo: Eddie and Robert Style 42
Dear Reader 45

WHERE ARE THEY NOW?

*I*n the early years of the AIDS epidemic, patients lingered on for months and sometimes, years, barely able to hold themselves erect. One day, quite out of the blue, a young man might experience uncontrollable watery diarrhea that continued every day until he died. Another might awaken and notice dark spots in his vision that progressed inexorably to blindness. From 1981 to 1995 there was little that could be offered these patients, at least of any lasting consequence. Most patients died in slow steps, sometimes in pain and often, alone.

The individuals in these stories are all dead with the exception of Tony and Gary who carry on, meeting their Saturday night obligations at the club.

One 82-year old patient who spent many years in Miami told me about his friends from clubs and bathhouses that died of the disease. He was diagnosed with HIV in the 1980's and struggled on with a devoted, uninfected younger partner. Even today they make do on Social Security checks, not very well, but happily. Old age is catching up to him though, he recently had a bypass of one of the arteries in his leg; one hip is bothering him and constipation is a major concern.

"I think I am a little demented too, Doc," Ralph said, "Tim needs to remind me about everything I do."

"No," I answer, "you're aging gracefully Ralph."

The patients in the stories that follow often lived chaotic lives. I used to ask myself what it was all about. Now, I accept the fact that they lived and enjoyed life, at least, for the short remainder of their lives. For many, the end came as a welcome relief from the draining anal ulcers, intractable diarrhea, creeping blindness, interminable weight loss and the next unknown complication just around the corner. They achieved a shred of dignity, sometimes for the first time in their lives, by choosing the manner of their death.

The epidemic came full circle the other day. Patty handed me the data sheets on a new patient named Ann who was twenty-one years of age. She sat in the examination room with her mother. "I was infected at birth," Ann said as I glanced at her laboratory values which were excellent. I turned to her mother,

"What regimen are you on?" I asked

The mother looked startled. "I'm not on anything. I adopted Ann at three years of age and a doctor called me out of the blue and said that I must test her for HIV. We did and she was positive and here we are twenty years later."

Ann was planning to marry. She came to ask about having a baby. I assured her that the baby would be born uninfected.

CLARK, THE FORERUNNER

I met Clark in his empty 5th floor wardroom. He stood at the threshold of his doorway as I approached. He was smiling sardonically. It was spring, 1984.

"Are you the doc that's supposed to know something?" he asked, breathing heavily.

"I was just looking at your chest x-ray. You have a severe pneumonia and you'll need intravenous antibiotics."

"Well you're gonna use pills. I'm not takin' anything i.v. I gotta get out of here. Look Doc, I know what's going on, I got AIDS, but I'm not going to change my fuckin' life. I'm not afraid of dying."

We walked into his room. The lights were off. I looked out the windows that faced west. By now it was almost dark and it would rain soon. Near the parking lot, Purple Martins were settling down in their multistoried house. Clark sat down on the edge of his bed and faced me with his arms akimbo, like wings, to assist in breathing.

"Alright but I've never treated anyone with this severe a pneumonia with oral drugs. I'm reluctant to do this," I said.

"That's all you're gonna use. Get me some oxygen while you're up."

"O.K. But no smoking!"

Clark put his hands behind him and leaned back. His pajama top, a light navy blue with 'VA' stenciled on the left chest pocket, fell open revealing his emaciated chest. His ribs retracted with every breath.

I walked back into one of the other wardrooms looking for a nurse to set up the oxygen. One elderly man, unshaven and ashen lay asleep in his bed. The other eight beds were empty with neatly tucked blankets and clipboards with blank vital signs sheets hanging from the foot of each bed frame. It was dark and it was lonely.

Just out of training myself, I had taken a position with the VA hospital and late one afternoon a Resident called me on the phone with a request to see "a forty-something male with a five-lobe pneumonia". The Residents caring for him thought he was impossible to deal with. The patient argued constantly and refused to comply with their demands not to smoke while receiving oxygen.

Cigarette smoke pervaded Clarks room. "Why don't you leave the interns and residents alone, Clark?" I asked.

"Those piss ants are always trying to *do* something instead of listening to me," he said.

Over the next six days Clark improved miraculously, shedding his nasal oxygen and breathing on his own. The dry cough subsided. He lost a further eight pounds. I met him standing in the same position at his door, this time with a smile. He was topless and one could see the muscle wasting of his shoulder girdles.

"I'm ready to go doc. I told you this wasn't going to get me," he said.

"I want you to stay on the antibiotics and see me in clinic in several days," I said.

"We'll see. I'm busy. Can't be bothered with a lot of this traveling back and forth shit."

I watched him get dressed. He was a small man even without the weight loss, maybe 5'8". He had coal-black, curly hair receding at his temples. His skin was an unhealthy looking white except where it was permanently red from the sun around the neck and forearms. The dark long hair on his chest and abdomen stood out in stark relief against the white skin.

I saw Clark in clinic the next week. He was still losing weight but was no longer short of breath or coughing.

"I'm back working at Radio Shack. At least I've got gas money. I even went back to my favorite rest stop on the Interstate. As long as

I'm not coughing I can hang around the toilet stalls. I must have given four blow jobs Friday night."

I came to know Clark through many clinic visits, dealing with his profanity and sarcasm. I could not understand what was in it for him hanging around Interstate rest stops. Often he was beaten after performing fellatio on fellow rest stop visitors.

He was an only son living with elderly parents who knew nothing about his life outside their home.

"Look, no one cared a shit about me when I was a kid. My parents were too old. By the time I was in junior high school I knew more about life than my Pop ever did. My folks are lost in their phony church. I knew I was queer, even when I was in grade school. I moved to New York City in the late seventies and had the time of my life, I tell you! God, I had hundreds of partners in one night."

"You know you could be passing this on to someone else."

"Well shit, I'm careful. Besides, do I give a fuck about anyone else?"

Clark started on AZT at massive doses. It made him anemic and weak. I saw him irregularly in a small clinic attended by two other HIV-infected patients. One of the patients had just been released from the state prison. He was a large man in his thirties who always wore overalls and a ball cap. The other man was in his middle forties and three years before had a back operation and was transfused with blood from an HIV-infected individual. He never missed an appointment and was accompanied by his wife. They sat in the waiting room with Clark. Invariably Clark prattled on with his bawdy stories. The wife was upset listening to Clark.

Clark continued with his complaints. "This shit is making me sick. I'm not going to take it any longer," He moved into a hospice that had just opened for HIV patients. Little was known about the disease at that time but several people got together to refurbish an old, abandoned house for patients dying of AIDS. A compassionate, effeminate parish priest from the leading cathedral in the city helped found the organization.

I saw Clark several weeks later in the clinic after his move. His complaints continued. He was still losing weight and the women attendants at the hospice were driving him nuts.

"I'm tired of listening to them talk about food and eating. Everything I eat, I just shit out in ten minutes. Can't they leave me alone? Can't they let me die on my own. One of them was saying that it was immoral of me not to eat. Please come down and talk to them, Doc."

It was around this time that I went to testify on behalf of the hospice at the City Council meeting. The Council was concerned that any hospice would eventually become a hub for illicit drugs. I said the hospice was essential for people infected with HIV.

Clark continued to plead on a daily basis. "Please Doc, come and tell these folks at the hospice to lay off. I have a right to do what I want. Why do I have to justify everything to them? They're threatening to move me out unless I do what they want,' complained Clark.

I went and spoke with the supervisor of the home, a woman in her thirties who was trying to answer to the needs of six men in the final stages of AIDS, all weak, all sick and all losing weight. I told her Clark's concerns and echoed his demand that he be allowed do as he pleased as long as he didn't get involved in illegal drugs and didn't disrupt the lives of the other hospice patients. She agreed.

Clark came and went as he pleased at the hospice for a further six months. One evening I received a telephone call and was told by a worker at the hospice that Clark had died, refusing to eat or drink during his final days.

MARIO THE PAINTER

*M*ario was an accomplished painter—his preferred medium was oil. Because of feigned helplessness he spent a good part of his life manipulating his family in perverse fashion. His family, with the exception of his father, always did what Mario wanted.

"Please, please help me, Doctor," the chubby, short Hispanic man said to me. He sported a four-day, spotty growth of beard. Perhaps "ratty" was a better description.

"Doctor, I'm so sick and the pain is intolerable. I need morphine, nothing else works," he pleaded spreading his arms wide with palms toward me. One could not help but notice his stained and irregularly shaped teeth. Mario was at least 50 pounds overweight which did little to enhance his appearance. His usual dress was an off-white T-shirt bulging at his flanks, un-pressed khaki trousers and scuffed white Nike shoes. The clinic receptionist thought he was a bum.

"Have you been taking your HIV meds, Mario?" I asked, dubious that I could trust his answer.

"Oh yes, Doktor, I do. Of course I do. I've had this disease for years and I wouldn't be alive if I didn't take my medicines. Ask my sister."

I looked toward Gloria. She was in her middle twenties, twenty years his junior. She had an honest face.

"Yes, Doktor. He takes all of his medicines, every day. The pain is really getting to him."

Mario's family was his universe. His father was overweening, his mother afraid of her husband and unable to speak a word of English. Gloria was often present when Mario came to clinic.

"Alright Mario, let's just get some lab tests and see where you are with this disease. I'll give you a script for some morphine. In several weeks we'll look at your lab values."

"Thank you. Thank you, Doctor,' Mario said.

I saw Mario two weeks later. He was carrying a large plastic sack with a rectangular object in it.

"Hello Doktor," Mario said. I brought you something. Maybe you'll like it. You don't have to accept it," he said as he pulled a 24 X 18" framed canvas painting out of the bag.

It was an oil painting, a still life of fruit in a bowl. I held it up at arms length.

"I think it's lovely," I said.

"I want you to have it," he said. "You are the only doctor who wants to help me."

"Well, I don't think you are taking your medicines, not all of them, Mario. I can tell from the lab results. You're going to have to do better," I said trying to get past the awkward appeal to my vanity. "I'll keep the painting and put it in my office today."

Mario came to clinic appointments every several months, filling his prescriptions in a desultory fashion except for the opiates, whose refill dates he never missed by more than a day. Sometimes Gloria left her work as a telephone operator to be present at the appointments to ensure her brother was treated respectfully.

Several years later Mario was painting full time. He taught a night class at the university on oil painting. Prints were made of many of his extant paintings. He proudly visited my office to keep me up to date on his accomplishments. His paintings were colorful landscapes of the desert with an affinity for cacti, especially the barrel cactus with its large, curved, fish hook-like spines. His palette was restricted to primary colors and great daubs of paint. He took a trip to Paris with a friend. He spoke French fluently and suggested some restaurants that I patronize next time I visited Paris.

One day Mario arrived in clinic and he could not look me in the eye. His deep brown eyes receded into their sockets. He was shamefaced. He informed me that he was bleeding from his rectum.

"Could you look at it?" he asked. His hair was disheveled. His mother accompanied him and was visibly trembling. Gloria could not get off work.

I pulled the curtain between his mother and the two of us. He lay against the examination table and pulled down his trousers and shorts. The latter were bloody and damp. I pulled on some gloves preparing to encounter more bleeding. Instead, protruding from the anus was a part of his bowel, swollen and engorged with blood, a prolapsed rectum.

"Doctor, I know it's a mess. This all began five years ago. My boyfriend broke into my house one evening with some of his friends and beat me and raped me. They used a toilet plunger handle in my anus. I needed a lot of surgery to repair what they did. Since then this happens sometimes. It's really scary when the bleeding starts."

After reinserting the prolapsed tissue, the problem resolved. Mario returned to his oil painting. He brought prints of his work and we put up more than 40 of them, scattered about the office.

Mario took enough of his HIV medicines to continue to live, but never enough or long enough to gain control of the virus.

Months later he came directly to my office after picking up his opiate prescriptions from the secretary and then knocked timidly on my door.

"Doktor? Doktor can you come and meet my father. He is out in the truck and he's angry because I need these drugs. He won't let my mother into the truck. He's just cursing her. He doesn't think I'm actually sick. Please, Doktor come and talk to him," he said gesturing for me to follow him.

I put on my white jacket and followed him out to the parking lot where his father was sitting behind the wheel of a white Ford 150 pickup. Mario's mother stood alongside the passenger side. She came up to me and squeezed my hand.

"Doktorr, por....favor," she said glancing sideways at her husband behind the wheel.

I walked around and introduced myself to Mario's father. He was coldly polite and obviously eager to leave. He was much smaller than Mario, even smaller than his wife. He was in his sixties with a ball cap pulled down to his ears and patches of dark hair protruding from beneath the cap. He had on a white T-shirt and blue jeans. I walked around to the passenger side to speak to Mario.

"Doctor, thank you for meeting him. He refused to let my mother back into the truck unless I really had a doctor. Now he will take us home. Thank you, Doktor," Mario said ecstatically. He helped his mother into the cab and got in behind her.

The following spring Mario came to the office and sat down in the chair facing my desk. He had something he wanted to say. He was smiling, happy, and heavier.

"Doktor, I have been working every day with my family in Mexico. I am welding parts on ironwork gates that we make for sale in Mexico and the States. My father is working alongside me. He says he forgives me. We work almost twelve hours a day. We have been living in Sonora for the past four months. I am finally making some money."

I was never to receive one of Mario's visits again.

A year later I was making rounds in the hospital and stumbled across Mario's name on the door of a 4th floor room. I peered into the room. He lay in a coma. He had been admitted for excruciating pain in his low back. He was heavily sedated and his scrotum was swelling, doubling its size each day. The pain was so severe and the sedation so heavy that he barely could rouse himself. The entire family was present, including Gloria. She told me that Mario had a new boyfriend. Everyone was gathered around his bed during the daylight hours. Weeks later Mario died, refusing chemotherapy and radiation therapy for an aggressive lymphoma that was eroding the bone in his spine and blocking lymph drainage from his legs and pelvis.

CAPTAIN HILL

Captain Hill came to clinic in his Army dress greens and waited silently in the waiting room while I saw several other patients. He told me his history: how he completed ROTC training, graduated from college, and once on active service recognized that he was gay. Like many men "coming out" he abandoned his conservative behavior and began visiting bathhouses on furloughs. He was "on the bottom" of thousands of sexual encounters over the next several years. He began to feel sick a year before I saw him. The day I saw him in clinic he was losing his eyesight in his left eye.

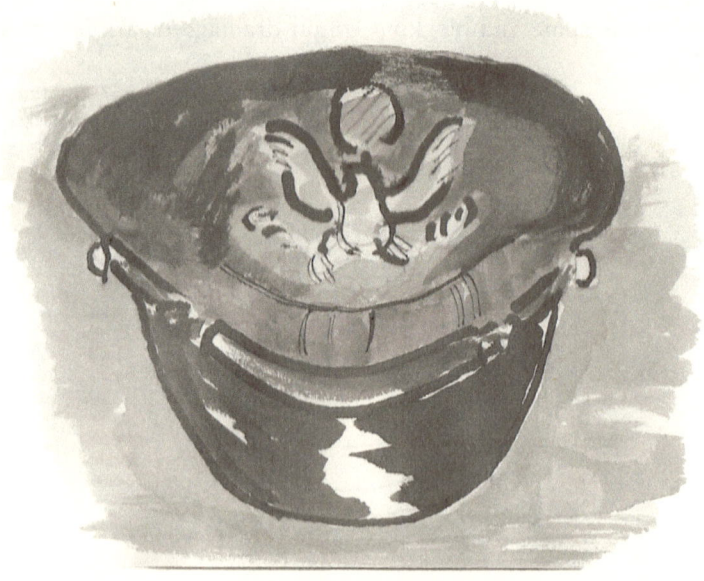

"Doc, I have blind spots in my vision. I don't understand what's happening," he said, staring straight ahead.

I looked at his eyes with the ophthalmoscope. He smelled of cologne. He had an impeccable haircut, his kinky hair trimmed to the shape of the skull. The pupils of his eyes were large and easily peered into. The retinas of both eyes were speckled with hemorrhages, some dangerously close to the macula, which if infiltrated with the viral disease would cost him his vision.

"It's a viral disease called CMV. We don't have any good therapy for this virus. The infection starts when the CD4 cell count is very low—we'll need to check your eyes frequently," I said.

Captain Hill was taking large amounts of AZT by mouth. Even this single drug led to some improvements in most patients for a couple of months. With the passage of time and only one drug, the virus eventually gained the upper hand.

He came back in six weeks. He had only a faint sensation of light and dark in his left eye. He was seeing less out of his right eye. There were extensive hemorrhages of both retinas. He walked out of the office with the aid of a slender white cane which he tapped against the walls.

He continued to attend the clinic in his Army dress greens with captain's bars on his shoulders. He wore a saucer cap with its large bronze eagle and yellow band across the front. Every piece of his clothing was "stracked away."

Later, his brother accompanied him to clinic after he could no longer see well enough to negotiate the hospital corridors. His brother was an identical twin and was living testimony to what Captain Hill would have looked like if he had not been infected with HIV. The brother stood by with a military bearing.

"Is it scary that you are losing your vision?" I asked Hill.

"No. I go to church on Sunday. I pray. I'm not afraid," he said.

He was now a phantom of his former self, thin, his face ravaged by loss of fat. His cheeks were heavily lined with creases.

I stumbled upon Captain Hill one more time. He was attending church one Sunday morning and I was driving on a rural road, bird watching. The sun was at its zenith overhead and the humidity was suffocating. In an opening among the pine trees I saw a white wood frame church with a short bell tower on the front facade. A sign at the roadside proclaimed that it was a Baptist church. There were a number of cars parked along the roadside. Captain Hill was standing alongside a white Cadillac convertible carefully placing his saucer cap on his head. His brother stood next to him and handed him his white cane. I drove on.

JON THE COQUETTE

*J*on seemed boyish even though he was in his thirties. His youthful appearance was enhanced by a flawless complexion and svelte body. This was all to change dramatically as he began to take antiretroviral medications. He eventually became something of a butterball, yet he retained his boyish look. He was a short man, five feet six inches tall and a great favorite of gay white and black men.

I first met him during one of his many stays on the 11th Floor psychiatric wing. Over the years he was hospitalized there on many occasions. Merely mumbling the words "I'm going to kill myself" to a young Intern on duty in the Emergency Room bought him a rapid pass to the 11th floor. Any admission usually signaled a stay of several weeks while Jon did his laundry, received visitors and entertained the other patients by playing the piano. In point of fact, Jon was much too fastidious to do anything to himself that would have risked death or disfigurement.

One day I was notified that he was back in the hospital. I took the elevator to the 11th floor. The desk clerk showed me into the dining room. Jon was seated at the upright piano effortlessly playing a tune by Scott Joplin. He swiveled around on the chair, glanced at me and politely stated,

"Hello, Doctor. How're you?"

"I've come to see you about the HIV. You'll need to start on some medicines. Your immunity is getting weaker and you're liable to be infected with some very bad diseases," I said.

We talked at length about HIV and how it affects the immune system. I drew some graphs and Jon asked questions. He seemed to grasp the severity of the problem. He was discharged on several antiretroviral medications as well as what became a pattern-- mood altering drugs that he used himself in haphazard fashion. Indeed, on future admissions he sometimes came in so over medicated that he couldn't talk or even lift his arm. He never took illicit drugs.

His admissions to the psychiatric unit occurred at times of great stress in his relationships with a parade of boyfriends.

"Colin is so angry with me," he said. "I really can't please him any more. There is nothing I can do. I took my antidepressants because everything seemed like a mess—I took too many."

Jon's right eye had a bruise below it and there was hemorrhaging into the sclera.

"He's not beating you up, is he?" I asked.

"Well…he gets angry. He threw a plate and hit me below the eye last week," Jon said.

"Get rid of the guy Jon," I said.

"I can't do that right now. We're sharing expenses on the apartment, pooling our checks. It's not that easy Doc."

I ran into Jon and his boyfriend, Colin, in the cafeteria. I saw the two of them seated in a booth talking. Colin was a surly looking white male in his early twenties who glowered at me over Jon's left shoulder.

I did not see Jon for another six months and by then he was on to a new boyfriend. By now his immune cells were as low as they could go. He was having trouble seeing out of one eye. I took the elevator to the 11th Floor and asked to be let into the Psychiatric wing. Jon lay in bed and refused to speak to me, staring at the wall and behaving as if he were paralyzed. Days later we talked and he agreed to begin on an intravenous medication for the CMV retinitis. The infection was severe and he would be blind in one eye, if not in both. We worked hard on preserving his vision in his remaining eye. He took his medicines only sporadically and then moved to live with his mother and sister in Oklahoma. I did not see him for a year.

Suddenly he was back on the 11th Floor, this time blind, and pounds heavier than I had seen him before. He sat at the piano and desultorily picked at the keys. He had lost much of his verve. He was frightened now because his current boyfriend Thomas was unlikely to stay on with him—a blind Jon was too much trouble to take care of. He and his boyfriend moved into a house not far from the hospital.

One day I found him in my office sitting quietly staring straight ahead. My secretary had seated him carefully in the sunlight. It was cold outside and he had a heavy Navy pea jacket on. I walked up behind him and noticed that his right cheek was swollen and reddened. There was an imprint of a clothes iron on his cheek with the tip towards his ear and the broad base down toward his chin.

Jon said to me, "Thomas was so angry with me 'cause I burned his shirt while ironing. He took the iron and pushed it against my face." Tears flowed down his cheeks. Raw, red skin showed where charred parts had peeled away from the edge of the burn.

"Did you call the police?" I asked.

"My sister called them. Thomas left me. Now I have no way to get around at all."

I saw Jon several times afterwards. He was tentative in his walking, terrified by his blindness. He never used a cane. The skin on his cheek healed in with a much darker color than his light brown skin. He wore his Navy pea jacket with the collar pulled up to partially hide the scar. His sister and mother moved him to Oklahoma. I heard later that he died at his sister's house.

LAUREN THE BLASPHEMER

There was shrieking from the examination room, a high-pitched nasal voice. After entering the room I was still not entirely certain of the sex of the patient. Lauren sat on the exam table with her legs crossed beneath her in a yoga position. She had on a sun bleached blue T-shirt. She had no discernible breasts. Her reddish blonde hair was cut like a flat top. She reached for a cigarette and started to light it.

"No smoking here," I said.

"You can't tell me what to do! I'll do what I want, God damn it" she said.

"Fine, but you won't be smoking in here."

Lauren began picking at several draining ulcers on her forearms. Her skin was wrinkled, plum colored and sun damaged and the rosacea about her nose and cheeks flared red.

I glanced at her medical record,

"It says here you've got quite a drug history: meth, heroin, crack…"

"Yea, but I don't shoot the shit up—I just smoke it and snort it, God damn it," she blurted out, fidgeting with her skirt, twisting the fabric and brushing at it with her hands. Her tennis shoes had holes in the fabric. She reached into her skirt pocket and removed the package of cigarettes again. I put my hand on her forearm.

"God damn it Doc! Let me do what I want," she shouted in her nasal high-pitched shrieking voice. Lauren drew back her skirt. She had no panties on. She spread her labia and pointed to a large abscess.

"There doc! That's the problem!" she shouted.

Hearing Lauren's shouting Patty came into the room wondering if she was needed. I gestured for her to take Lauren to the laboratory for some blood tests.

In the years of caring for Lauren she never had any cellular immunity to speak of. When not high on drugs she promised to take her HIV medications, but her resolve was weak. Within several weeks she would slip out of contact, only to return months later thinner, sicker and weaker than before.

I had not seen Lauren for a year when the Emergency Room called one day wondering if I would come and "deal" with Lauren. She was shrieking profanities at the ER clerks and the doctors and she refused to leave the premises without pain medications. I said I'd come over.

"She's outside on the sidewalk," the clerk informed me.

I walked through the automatic glass doors out into the sunshine. Lauren was lying on her back in the middle of the sidewalk with her feet toward me and one leg crossed over her raised knee. She had no panties on. Her skirt had slipped up around her waist. Smoke was billowing up above her. Pedestrians walked past her recumbent figure.

"Lauren, put your legs down and sit up," I said.

"Oh, hi Doc. I really need some pain pills. The Goddamn ER won't give 'em to me." She threw a lit cigarette butt toward the building and sat up.

I gave her a script for some medication and told her to be in clinic on Tuesday.

Lauren's family had been dealing with her problems for over twenty years, ever since her late teen years.

"Doc, can't you just admit her for several days. My wife is exhausted and my other daughter is losing her patience and won't let her stay with her. A weekend of her yelling and suffering with pain—we're not going to do it anymore," her father confided to me on the phone. Fortunately, Social Services came to their rescue. Lauren was moved to an apartment that same day after signing numerous documents stipulating her forcible removal from the apartment if she were found to be using illicit substances.

After moving to an apartment Lauren began coming to clinic weekly and even started HIV medications. She came to clinic thinly clad, but it was evident that she was showering and preparing meals in her apartment. True to form, just when everything appeared to be going well, a urine drug screen came back positive. She lost her domicile and was back out on the streets.

After multiple repetitions of chaste behavior followed by orgies of drugs there came a time when Lauren showed up at clinic and announced that she wanted nothing done for her anymore. All she wanted was something for diarrhea. She was so thin that she looked like an insubstantial bird. The skin around her cheeks and nose was magenta in hue and she had open wounds on her forearms.

The police found her dead in an abandoned building several weeks later.

THE JEWEL BOX

Lieutenant Dickson was tall, thin and elegant with dark skin like a Sudanese. His smile showed off his large, handsome teeth and he sported a meticulously trimmed thin moustache. He shaved just so, down to a single hair. He paid little attention to any of my instructions about taking his antiretroviral medications. His elegant form always made a stir amongst the men in the waiting room when he left. Dickson dressed in dark trousers with a thin black belt, white dress shirts and cufflinks with large colorful stones. Teola, our nurse, approved of his dress even though he was a bit vain.

We saw Dickson infrequently over the years and he always attended clinic with a companion. He was the talk of the waiting room amongst the gay men. Teola despaired of him ever following any of our instructions.

On one visit he complained of skin lesions on his arm. I looked carefully at his forearms. Kaposi's sarcoma lesions were emerging on his left wrist. We discussed the problem and I suggested he see a radiation oncologist if the lesions continued to enlarge. He pulled the sleeve down over the lesions, fastened his cufflink and left.

Several months later he returned. This time there were visible purplish lesions on the back of his left hand. He complained that his vision was failing in his right eye. I looked carefully with the ophthalmoscope and there was extensive CMV retinitis. He refused intravenous therapy for the infection as he claimed it would impede his lifestyle.

"I go to clubs every night of the week. People see me, buy me drinks and food. I am not going to show up with an i.v. in my arm," he said. He walked out of clinic with his male escort.

Months later I saw Dickson wearing the same dark blue trousers, but now they were a little soiled at the pockets. The white shirt was worn at the cuff. He could not see details out of either eye. He stood proudly in the examination room with his back straight and chin out. His gaze was vacant, but he listened to my questions. The KS lesions on his forearm had now enlarged to bulbous growths. He could easily feel them now. This depressed him because he knew they were visible to others. He was escorted to the club each evening, but the old pattern of being the center of attention no longer occurred. He lamented the drastic change and wondered what he could do.

I asked him to write down for me what his life was like and bring it to his next appointment. I then handed him a black marker and a packet of paper. He could make out the dark marker on white paper.

He came to clinic a month later and handed me several sheets of paper smudged with dirt and ink. He had written with a marker in a quavering hand:

> ...It used to be when I walked into the Jewel Box every man turned to stare at me. I was that beautiful! They couldn't wait to talk to me. I always had two boyfriends, one on each side. I never bought my own drink.
>
> Now, I'm nobody. Cancer's eating me up. I can't see anymore. I sit alone at a table. Friends don't come around so often...

Dickson now came every week to clinic. Sarcomatous growths were visible on all of his limbs. The skin on his arms became scaly giving it a grayish cast that contrasted sharply with the still beautiful complexion of his thin, hollow cheeks which he was careful to cover with an emollient each morning. His eyes became exceedingly prominent as the weight loss continued. He began to look terrified like a figure in a Goya painting. He told me that his companions would take him to the club at night and leave him at his favorite table and pick him up hours later. He rarely spoke with anyone at the club any more. He enjoyed inhaling the smoke of others and listening to the music and banter amongst the customers at the bar.

Like many of the patients in those times, there was no sharp ending, no obituary. We heard through the grape vine that Dickson had died.

REVEREND STEVEN, TELE-EVANGELIST

"Doctor, I brought Ardis in because she's not doing well... losing weight...having fevers. I'm her pastor," the black man of forty said to me. He was dressed in a cheap, two-piece, cerulean blue polyester suit. He had on a broad red tie, white socks and white suede shoes.

"I have taken her into my house for the past couple of months," the Reverend said.

Ardis had immigrated from Africa five years before and at that time had a negative HIV test. She looked askance during the entire examination and spoke in a whisper. I had to lean toward her in order to hear her responses. The Reverend repeated most of her statements. I explained that she needed to start on antiretroviral medications immediately. The Reverend exhorted her with, "God will help you through this...The Church is behind you..."

I saw Ardis a few more times and we could never address where she had contracted the HIV infection for the want of privacy. Pastor Steven was always at her side. She died suddenly of a heart attack after being rushed to the hospital several months later. Steven assured me that the Church would take care that a proper burial ensued.

One evening late at night, months later, I was surfing TV channels when I suddenly came upon Reverend Steven addressing the TV audience. Yes, there he was on the Access channel in all the splendor of his blue two-piece suit and white suede shoes.

"We welcome everyone to our Church of Christ…"

He ended the telecast with, "Be blessed by our telecast." His trousers appeared blowsy and his face, puffy.

Months later Steven came to the clinic. "I have HIV, and I don't know how I got it," he said. "It must be from helping my parishioners."

He had gained thirty pounds. On examination it was evident why. He had pitting edema to his hips. His lower extremities were encased in fluid that his kidneys could not get rid of. The workup disclosed that he had glomerulonephritis brought on by the HIV infection. He began appropriate medications and improved.

"I feel so good that I'm not even tired after my TV show," he confided to me. "I am able to preach my usual two hours on Sunday. For a while I couldn't do it."

Reverend Steven never took his medications on a daily basis nor on time. He frequently came to clinic with his legs encased in edema. He couldn't get his shoes tied. He did so poorly with his HIV drugs that he soon had resistant virus requiring frequent medication changes.

At every visit to the clinic he said, "I'm so thankful to God for the good fortune I have had…I praise God every day and ask God that I continue as pastor for my Church." Later he was hospitalized on multiple occasions, and finally placed in a nursing home. Reverend Steven's Church of Christ ceased to exist.

I visited the Reverend Steven in the nursing home located just behind the clinic. I walked through creosote bush and cholla cactus to reach the side door of the facility.

Reverend Steven was on the third floor lying in bed. The edema was severe, now, up to his waistline.

"Hi, Doc," he said, not moving his limbs or head. I squeezed his hand. He was too weak to raise his head. He was refusing to take any of his medications.

"God is calling me," he said. The nursing home employee stood by his bedside with a disapproving look on her face.

WAYNE: THE MAN WHO WOULD NOT EAT

I had seen Wayne years before in the clinic and did not remember him when I encountered him this time. Now, he was as thin as a rail and his speech was weak, almost a whisper. His mother brought him to the appointment.

Wayne was thirty-five years old, perhaps 5 feet 10 inches tall and weighed ninety-five pounds. His black-rimmed eyeglasses appeared too large for his face. He had to continuously push on the bridge of the glasses to keep them on his nose. His face was covered with a scraggly beard, little circular tufts of curly white hair scattered randomly about on his cheeks. His upper arms were little bigger than large carrots. His walk was halting and he could barely pick his feet up off the ground. He wore faded blue jeans and white gym shoes.

Wayne didn't want to take any medications—he had been refusing to do so for several years. His mother was in the examination room, upset because Wayne made sudden demands upon her to provide him with a cheeseburger or a milk shake and he wanted them immediately. He refused to eat the meals she carefully prepared for him three times a day. His mother was adamant that Wayne pick up his bedroom.

"Things smell in his room," she said.

In addition to these difficulties brought on by Wayne, his mother was very ill as well, with advanced diabetes and heart failure. I reserved my commiserations for the mother, rather than Wayne since he was oblivious to my suggestions. I was convinced that Wayne had only days to live at the present rate he was going. It did not seem possible that he could even be alive at this time.

The very limited examination that Wayne allowed me to perform demonstrated the most extensive case of thrush I had ever seen. Over his entire soft palate there was an off-white membrane that could not be dislodged with a tongue blade. It was so chronic that it had a leathery feel to it. I wondered why he would not take a pill that would cure this in several days.

"I'm going to get better on my own," he whispered.

Several weeks later Wayne's sister came to talk to me about Wayne and her mother. She worked in the office of the juvenile court across the street from the clinic. She was solicitous of Wayne and was concerned about her mother. She thought that her mother's health was failing rapidly and wondered how she could continue taking care of Wayne. Wayne lived in one bedroom in his mother's house. No one except Wayne could enter his bedroom. He had some of his favorite foods secreted away in his wardrobe. He would appear in the kitchen most mornings and have a short talk with his mother then retire to his room to nap or go to the living room and watch TV. His mother would go out on her own in a taxi to purchase special treats for Wayne when he asked for them. By the time the food was brought back to him, Wayne usually had forgotten what he couldn't live without and made no attempt to eat it. This occurred several times a week and was slowly crushing his mother's spirit. Wayne's mother was obsessed with worry that Wayne would fall asleep smoking and burn the house down. Several times she had come into the living room and discovered a smoldering cigarette in the carpet and Wayne fast asleep in his reclining chair.

His Mother brought Wayne to clinic one other time and talked at length about how Wayne refused to eat. I looked at his mouth again and the same leathery whitish membrane coated his entire soft palate.

"He just won't eat anything Doctor. I try and give him Ensure, but he refuses," she said.

"Tell her it's my business, not hers," Wayne said slowly raising his right arm and waving it at his mother with a deprecating look on his face. His fingernails were long and curled and dirt was visible beneath them. He had tobacco stains on his right second and third fingers and the dark skin was yellow at the distal phalanges. I placed my hand on his knee, it was now the size of a man's elbow. I pleaded with him to take some antifungal medication for the thrush, but Wayne said, "No!"

One afternoon Wayne's sister came to the clinic without an appointment and very distressed. She had a beautiful black and crimson silk scarf around her shoulders and a black dress—dressed impeccably in contrast to Wayne. She informed me that her mother had suddenly died and now someone had to take care of Wayne who was still living in his mother's house. She arranged for Wayne to stay in a nursing home not far from the clinic. I promised to visit him every couple of weeks. I could not fathom how he had outlived his mother.

As I had promised his sister I looked in on him at the nursing home. It was a short trek over to the building from the clinic. I knew Wayne would barely acknowledge me, perhaps he'd deny he knew me. He lay in the bed. He was much weaker than when I had last seen him, if that were possible. I leaned over toward him to listen to his just audible whisper,

"I want my cigarettes, Doc," he said.

I engaged in some purposeless conversation and listened to the nurse go on about Wayne's lack of trying to eat and always trying to smoke. I left the nursing home, walking across a field to the hospital. Wayne died the next week.

EDDIE AND THE 7TH STREET BRIDGE

Of all the HIV-positive patients that I ever cared for, Eddie possessed the most beautiful smile. His skin was dark black, his teeth large and white with one of his upper incisors encased in gold. He usually had a cigarette dangling from his lips. He wore blue jeans without a belt and white short-sleeved T-shirts with the sleeves carefully rolled up several turns.

He was invariably late for appointments and I would walk down to the smoking lounge, take a big breath, enter the smoke-filled room, look around rapidly, and gesture for him to follow me. Since I was a former smoker, I felt justified in berating him over this habit.

"OK Doc, let me just finish this puff or two. I'm coming," he said rising from the naugahyde covered chair.

I got to know Eddie in 1995 just prior to the use of multiple, highly effective anti-retroviral drugs. He had no cell-mediated immunity. His CD4 cell count came back "0" on his blood draws. He had long since stopped taking any of his medications. Now he was losing weight rapidly. An infection with a fungus common in the Midwest was diagnosed. He was dying of histoplasmosis. He agreed to come to clinic twice a week to receive an intravenous drug. I was hoping we could keep him alive long enough to convince him to use the new antiretroviral drugs that were just coming into use in the clinic.

"I promise to be here twice a week," Eddie said smiling to Gretchen, my assistant. It was summer and he wore a freshly ironed white T-shirt and blue jeans, the latter kept up now with a white plaited leather belt. He was going to stay with a friend who would help him make his appointments.

Over the next two months Eddie never missed a clinic visit or his dose of intravenous antifungal. He began to gain weight and his fevers occurred less often. His health was clearly improving.

One day Eddie came into clinic very late, Gretchen was wondering how he would be able to receive the drug fast enough so that he could still get back home before dark. I came to talk to him. His white T-shirt was filthy and his normally impeccably creased blue jeans were stained with soot. The one gold tooth flashed in his mouth and a smile from ear to ear appeared on his face.

"I have a place under the 7th Street Bridge now. I used to like to stay there all day. Now I'm living there," he said.

The 7th Street viaduct passed over the Kansas River. It was a heavily traveled artery that was a tangle of concrete on- and off-ramps. It required no small amount of agility to walk from beneath the bridge across the high-speed roadways to nearby housing areas. There was little or no vegetation on the river near the bridge. Not far distant was the point at which the Kansas River debouched into the Missouri.

"I have a small cardboard house under the bridge. I've collected a lot of junk that people threw out, a chair, a sofa. I'm looking for an old refrigerator so I can store things in it and lock up. It's nice watching the water go by. I'm happy there," he said.

"Just don't miss your drug infusions," Gretchen said.

Over the following year Eddie came to clinic in a fairly regular fashion to receive intravenous infusions of the antifungal. He continued to live under the bridge collecting trinkets and odds and ends to complement his cardboard structure. The city police finally rooted him from his home site and placed him in a boarding house nearby the hospital. We began to see less and less of him.

A police officer came to the clinic one afternoon. "We were called to the boarding house because no one had seen Eddie for weeks in the building. There was an odor coming from his room. We broke in," the officer said. They found Eddie in his jeans and T-shirt and decomposed to such a point that when his body was removed, part of the mattress came with him.

DEBBIE, ROBERT AND STIMPY

"Do you think I've got HIV, Doc?" the middle-aged woman sitting on the examination table asked me. She had long, straight red hair, a low cut blouse and Bermuda shorts.

"I'm pretty sure that's what's going on," said her boyfriend standing next to me. He was a muscular man of medium height who drove 18-wheelers for a living. "I stopped my meds several months ago. I've seen this all before."

Debbie was having difficulty swallowing solid foods, experiencing night sweats and losing weight. This was the second girlfriend of Robert's that I had seen in the last eight years. Robert insisted she come to our clinic since he was convinced that she had contracted HIV—he was right. Debbie was endoscoped and shown to have esophageal candidiasis. The tests were positive for HIV.

Treatment of the esophageal infection quickly restored her appetite and the acute phase of the HIV infection subsided. Debbie said nothing about the manner in which she contracted HIV. She had been divorced for years and had two grown daughters whom she occasionally saw. She recently met Robert after he was released from prison. He shortly thereafter moved into her rural home. They kept several horses and a dog named Stimpy.

Robert restarted his HIV medications and Debbie eventually needed them as well. They came to clinic as a couple. At every visit they showed color prints of Stimpy, a Mexican hairless pup. Stimpy was ugly, with enormously outsized eyes and a small bulbous cranium. He often stayed in the car while the two were in clinic. Patty, the clinic nurse, pinned his photographs up over her workspace—it was surprising the number of patients we had with Chihuahuas and Mexican hairless dogs. Following each visit Patty accumulated more and more photos of Stimpy. There was Stimpy standing before the grandchildren. There was Stimpy walking with a mincing gait in front of the horses. He was small enough to fit into a woman's handbag.

Several years after Debbie's acute infection she confided to me her anger and sense of betrayal by Robert, meaning his having infected her knowingly with HIV. They were still together and she didn't want to openly confront him over the issue. Robert had been in prison for drunk driving in the past and just recently lost his license again. Stimpy and the couple used taxis to come to clinic. Debbie was having a great deal of difficulty with her HIV medications whereas, Robert responded rapidly to drugs and controlled the infection. Debbie was using increasing amounts of methadone for joint aches and pains. I began to see her less and less. Her usual *joie de vive* disappeared.

One day the couple came to clinic. Debbie was sobbing uncontrollably.

"Robert and I were sitting on the verandah having a drink Sunday afternoon and Stimpy was snooping around in the flower garden. We were talking and all of a sudden there was a high-pitched scream. We looked up and Stimpy was leaping straight up in the air," Debbie choked back a gasp.

"He fell down plumb dead on the spot," said Robert. "He was bitten by a Mojave rattlesnake. He was dead within seconds."

After Stimpy's death Debbie declined rapidly and stopped taking her medications. Robert returned to prison for five years. Debbie lost 30 pounds of weight and died alone.

BUCKAROO WITH A SHAPELY BOTTOM

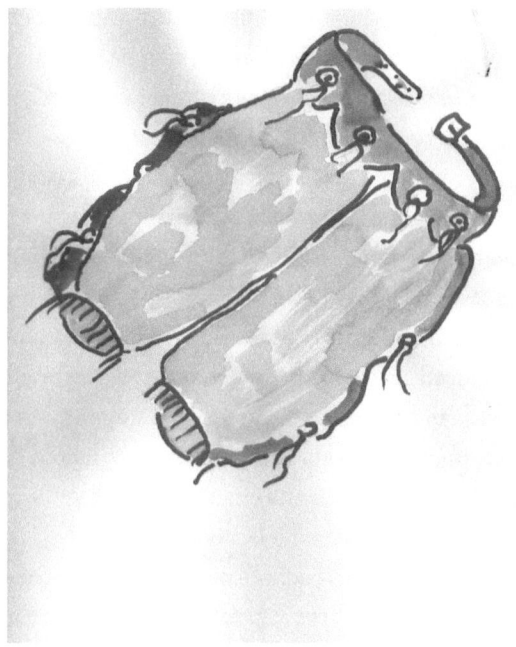

The Jewel Box during the 1980s and 90s was located on Main Street at a spot now occupied by a Wendy's. Formerly it had been located on Troost Avenue and was known throughout the Midwest as place where drag at its finest was to be found. Several bars in New York and LA were its only rivals. Truman Capote and Rock Hudson could be found in the Jewel Box's audience. It was the place to be, with three daily shows. After moving to Main Street the burlesque acts were replaced with pantomime.

Randal had many appearances at the Jewel Box and usually to great acclaim. He was a short man, 35 years of age with closely cropped dark brown hair. The hair at his temples was waxed and brushed up giving his tonsure a flat top look. He was extremely muscular as I learned doing a physical examination at his first visit to the clinic. He was the first of many patients I saw over the years that made a fetish of working out daily. His entire body was evenly tanned including the buttocks. He possessed large, well-defined biceps, a small waist with taut abdominal musculature and no body hair. He was squeamish about having his blood drawn because he feared that he might faint. He was a great favorite of my assistant Gretchen and always kept her up to date on his acting success.

Gretchen showed me a series of photos taken of Randal performing at the Jewel Box that she had taken. A plush red stage curtain could be seen in the background and Randal was walking onto the stage. His torso had several leather bands crossing his abdomen with chains going over his shoulders. His skin was glistening and below the waist he had light-colored leather cowboy chaps and cowboy boots. In a series of photos Randal pirouetted across the stage and the last photo showed him facing the curtain. He was entirely naked with several leather straps that buckled on the chaps at mid thigh. His head was turned in profile and he flashed a lascivious grin.

Shortly before the AIDS cocktail of drugs became the standard of therapy Randal went on a short trip to New York where he appeared onstage in Brooklyn and the Bronx. Upon his return home he was very ill, short of breath and within days placed on a ventilator. We could not figure out what the cause of his pulmonary failure. I visited him on several occasions and noted the black VA logo on the pajamas that covered Randal's marvelous physique. He died after two weeks on the ventilator.

TONY AND GARY

Tony was the reigning Drag Queen in the city. He was also impresario of a drag show staged weekly at a local bar. His entry as Cher in a white slinky gown down to his ankles was the highlight of the evening. Gary, Tony's long time partner was, improbable as it seemed, a bull rider who dressed Tony for his acts.

They came as a couple to clinic and always with loud bickering between the two in the waiting room.

Patty, our nurse said in an aside as she put them in the examination room, "This pair's going to be difficult." She put both of them in the same examination room.

Tony was in his late thirties with straight black hair worn in a ponytail and carefully plucked, black eyebrows composed in broad arcs. Gary was a morbidly thin man, the same age as Tony, dressed in Wranglers that were bunched up about his cowboy boots. He invariably sported a silver and gold belt buckle he had won riding Brahma bulls, a cowboy shirt with snap buttons up the front and a heavily worn ball cap with a tattered bill that he pulled tightly over his skull.

"When did you learn that you were positive Tony?" I asked.

"Maybe a year ago, but we just learned about Gary last month. I'm having a helluva time getting him to eat. He's starvin' to death and the more he loses weight the more difficult he is to live with."

"Oh my ass! You're just raggin' on me all the time. That's the problem," Gary said frowning at Tony.

Tony shot back with, "See! Wha'd I tell you Doc? Irritated, anxious, short-tempered. That's Gary."

"Okay, let's quit here and I'll deal with the two of you separately," I said.

Both needed to begin antiretroviral medications. They did so and had excellent responses—the virus becoming undetectable within several months.

Tony brought in a signed 10 X 12 inch glossy glamour shot of himself as Cher in a local drag contest.

"You see, I don't get any credit," said Gary, "even though I do all of the hard work before the show begins. I shave his legs, apply the wax and do all of the facial makeup."

Tony smiled showing his perfect, large white teeth. "It's kinda true," he said.

Tony came to clinic with his mother on one occasion, both of them looking tired and worried. Gary had been missing for days. The last time he was seen, he was driving some of Tony's friends in a recently purchased Lexus sedan. Tony's mother was convinced that something awful had happened to Gary. Tony was nearly in tears. He called the police, but they could do little.

The Lexus was found parked in a cotton field in the next county. Gary was locked in the trunk, delirious from dehydration and the heat. He didn't recover consciousness for several days. Gary claimed to have been injected with illicit drugs until he was in a stupor. He missed his antiretroviral medications for over a week and for the first time had a measurable viral load in his blood samples.

Gary became the center of attention. Tony's mother fawned over Gary. He acted peculiarly for several days, wobbling when he walked and slurring his speech. He eventually improved.

"Thank God!" said Tony, "I was so worried those assholes had killed him."

Gary swore that he was going to hunt down his two kidnappers and kill them.

"By God, he'll do it too," said Tony. "He's a cousin of Anne Franke and a member of the Jewish mafia. I hope he doesn't go on with this."

Gary eventually lost his anger and ceased his plans of revenge. Both of their lives returned to the mundane: worrying about Tony's complexion and Gary's appetite. The nightclub routine took precedence and their customary bickering was resumed during their clinic visits.

Several years later Gary and Tony were struggling in their relationship. They separated, moving several houses away from one another. They still walked together each evening. Gary occasionally went to Tony's house and ironed Tony's shirts.

Tony's mother expressed her allegiance to Tony and now her distrust of Gary. "I don't trust that bastard Gary! He doing drugs and he's going to drag Tony down with him," she said scowling.

The two men continued to come to clinic together. Tony usually sat comfortably in the chair and informed me of Gary's "state of affairs". "Well, he has a lot of headaches. He needs all of these narcotics and I'm having some sort of skin problem on my face."

Gary usually aroused himself from a stupor and slurred something to the effect of, "Tony is just bitchin' again. Always complaining about something I'm doing."

I learned over years of through many such visits to pat them the two on the back and pronounce, "You guys are doing great. Keep up the good work." Gary and Tony come to clinic twice a year now.

SON OF A BITCH EMMIT

*E*mmit was the angriest patient I ever knew. He was approaching forty years of age and had spent the last five years in Leavenworth federal prison. Prior to his incarceration he spent fifteen years dealing and using drugs on the street. Now, out of prison and penurious he could only occasionally obtain heroin. He came to clinic sporadically and only when he had an infection related to drug injection.

He was a man of violent gestures and language and had nothing but disdain for healthcare workers, except for Teola, my assistant, who was unafraid of him. She spoke to him in a direct, uncompromising fashion informing him that he was going "to behave like any other patient or leave!"

Emmit was over six foot four inches tall and emaciated from longstanding AIDS. He only intermittently took his medications and of course, the failing regimen was blamed entirely on the incompetence of his physicians. During one visit he complained to me of black spots in his visual fields. I looked carefully at his retinas with the ophthalmoscope. His left eye had evidence of extensive CMV retinitis close to the fovea, the central vision spot. He refused to allow anyone to put in a catheter and begin a drug that would arrest the process of his declining vision.

"I told you I was going blind" he shouted, "and you did nothun'. I wanna speak to the hospital director, he'll get rid of your ass."

Teola could hear his voice rising to a high pitch. She came swiftly into the examination room.

"Alright Emmit, that's enough. Get your shirt on and come out here in the waiting room," she said. Teola then set up a visit to the ophthalmologist and a return visit to the clinic.

Several weeks later I saw Emmit standing in the waiting room, this time appearing uncertain as to which direction to go. Teola guided him into an examination room by his elbow.

"Goddamn you Doc! I'm going blind and it's because of you, you sorry shit. I want something done about this, now!" Emmit barked at me.

I explained the therapy to him again and he refused once again. I informed him that he definitely would go blind if he didn't allow us to give him intravenous medications.

The next time I saw Emmit he came to clinic in manacles, escorted by County Sheriff's Officers. He was in custody awaiting trial for drug dealing and battery.

"Goddamn you Doc!" he greeted me in his usual fashion. I'm blind and it's all your fault. If I weren't in handcuffs, I'd kill you!" The presence of the guards allowed me to overcome any fears I had of him. Later, however, I began to worry that they would let him out and he would show up at clinic on his own with a weapon.

Emmitt had not taken any of his medicines since going to prison because the guards confiscated all of his HIV meds. I wrote out a short letter asking the prison personnel to reinstate his medications. I placed the letter in an envelope.

"You're the asshole that made me go blind," he shouted as he was escorted out of the examination room for the last time.

Teola approached me after Emmit had been escorted to the prison vehicle. She had an envelope in her hand. "What is this for?" she asked.

"A useless script for Emmit, Teola. It can wait till his next visit, I guess."

There was no next visit, Emmitt died in the county jail.

KENDO: EDDIE AND ROBERT STYLE

Eddie was in his late thirties and had something of the cherub about him. He was over six feet tall but retained an adolescent plumpness and childish demeanor. He was flamboyantly gay. He had many affectations and they often changed between clinic visits. One day he began to use a cane. Eddie's cane was large and heavy with an iron ferrule at the tip. It sported a gently curved bronze handle nicely worked in a snakeskin motif. Eddie was fond of scarves and allowed one end to hang elegantly from his shoulder that he occasionally flicked dramatically for emphasis during his conversation.

When I first encountered Eddie, he was living with his mother in a suburb. Later he moved to Midtown with a boyfriend. Eddie and his boyfriend quarreled constantly. On one occasion in winter Eddie came to clinic in a heavy overcoat and slumped into a chair in the clinic waiting room. He was without his cane. He and his boyfriend had fought in their apartment and the police were called in by the neighbors. Eddie and his boyfriend were evicted. Now Eddie had nowhere to go. His face was lacerated and bruised.

Later Eddie met Robert, a short, stocky, studious looking man very involved in promoting all things African: clothing, kufis and greeting cards. He wore gold-rimmed circular eyeglasses like James Joyce. I never saw Robert without his yellow kufi adorned with brown vertical bars. Only later when he was ill, and in the hospital, did I realize why he never parted with the kufi. He had very prominent frontal baldness and the kufi covered his scalp nicely.

Whenever Eddie had an appointment in clinic, there was Robert; and whenever Robert had an appointment in clinic, there was Eddie. They seemed genuinely loving comrades. Robert put up with Eddie's flamboyant actions in the Jewel Box at night and seemed comfortable standing by and observing Eddie's narcissistic behavior. On the other hand, Eddie seemed content to listen to Robert's sometimes withering and rambling comments about his behavior as well as his cavalier approach to treating HIV. Robert was now wearing African scarves to clinic along with his kufi and using a thin, black, wooden cane.

Each year we invited patients to a Christmas party held in the cafeteria in the afternoon. Usually fifty or more patients attended for several hours. All of us gathered in the chapel before making our way to the cafeteria. One after another of the participants walked to the chapel lectern and read the names of patients who had died during the previous year. Teola placed a red ribbon for each deceased patient on a miniature Christmas tree. I provided a brief summary of where science was in the battle against HIV. During my presentation I noticed that Robert and Eddie were not sitting with one another. Eddie sat in the rear with both hands clutching the head of his cane, beret on his scalp and a long dark overcoat and blue scarf wrapped tightly around his neck. Robert sat in the front pew with his kufi just so and his thin cane leaning against the kneeling rail in front of him.

At the Holiday Party things started going awry. The food line was forming alongside one wall. Robert and Eddie were in line near one another and both had dressed for the cold weather with long overcoats although the room was quite warm. Suddenly one of the patients shouted,

"Look out!"

Robert and Eddie had raised their canes and were striking at one another. The clacking of the impacting canes resounded in the room.

"You fop, Eddie. Stop this nonsense," said Robert as he adjusted his eyeglasses.

"Goddamn you, Robert," Eddie shouted, "I'm sick of putting up with your shit."

Teola maneuvered her body between the two of them and broke up the encounter.

"Now everyone get back in line and get their cake," Teola said.

Later Eddie moved several hundred miles away to stay in his mother's summer home on the Lake of the Ozarks. He took a new boyfriend with him. One summer day Eddie arrived at the clinic in shock and incapable of giving a coherent history. He had removed a tick from his forearm several weeks before and had been picking at the site constantly. There was an open ulceration on his forearm oozing a dishwater-like liquid. A culture from the site grew *Staphylococcus* and several days later he was covered from head to foot with the intense rash of toxic shock. Several days in the ICU brought him back to life. He left the hospital weaker and thinner. I never saw Eddie in clinic again.

Robert suffered from a painful, slow growing tumor of his anal region caused by a virus. He had multiple excisions of the growth with little success. Usually the lesion went into "remission" when he took all of his prescribed antiretroviral medications. He moved to a rural area of Kansas and I did not hear from him again.

DEAR READER

You may ask yourself, "Why are these people's lives so full of chaos and violence?"

I offer you the following tentative explanation. In the Eighties when the epidemic began, little was known by society at large about gay men. The gay culture came to prominence with the onset of the epidemic. One man after another was informed that there was little to be done for their deadly disease. They would surely die at some point in the future and then, most likely, emaciated and unable to breathe. It would be another decade before accurate prognostications about the disease could be made by physicians. In the meantime, each patient knew only that death was imminent and nothing could change the outcome. At the time there was a waning belief in religious solutions to confronting death, a credo of "you only live once" and, most importantly, a failure of technology to turn the epidemic around. It is no wonder that drugs, sex, and violence were a prominent part of the final phases of these patient lives.

In thinking back over the lives of the patients I have written about, and even, to this day, think about, daily, I am reminded by some lines of Ezra Pound describing One who suffered and didn't complain, not unlike the men and women of the Jewel Box Biographies:

> He cried no cry when they drave the nails
> And the blood gushed hot and free,
> The hounds of the crimson sky gave tongue
> But never a cry cried he

—Ezra Pound, *Ballad of the Goodly Fere*

www.ingramcontent.com/pod-product-compliance
Lightning Source LLC
Chambersburg PA
CBHW021452070526
44577CB00002B/376